The Last Girl

for Alli

ACKNOWLEDGMENTS

For their encouragement and support, I would like to thank the following
journals, in which these poems first appeared:

Maudlin House: "Whatever it Takes to Fit into Our Calvin Klein Jeans, 1981"
Roi Faineant: "Blades"
DarkWinter Lit: "A Poem is the Chelsea Hotel"
The Hooghly Review: "Ode to My Father's Marlboro Lights" and "Ritual Lost"
HAD: "Self-Portrait in Things My Sisters Told Me Not to Do, but I Did
     Anyway"
Five Minutes: "For Eight Weeks" published in prose form as "Not My
     Doctor"

Publisher: Leah Huete de Maines
Editor: Christen Kincaid
Cover Art: M.R. Mandell
Author Photo: Matt Kallish
Cover Design: Elizabeth Maines McCleavy

Order online: www.finishinglinepress.com
          also available on amazon.com

Author inquiries and mail orders:
Finishing Line Press
PO Box 1626
Georgetown, Kentucky 40324
USA

Contents

daughters

The Father Drives Me Home 1

Waiting for My Father in the Lobby of the Disneyland Hotel 2

My First Name is Margaret 3

Ode to My Father's Marlboro Lights 5

When I Was Sixteen, I Realized My Parents Were No Longer

    in Love 6

The Day My Mother Disappeared 7

Snow Globe 8

Our Apartment Downtown 9

My Champion 10

For Eight Weeks 11

sisters

Benefits of Being the Black Sheep 15

Self-Portrait in Things My Sisters Told Me Not to Do, but I

    Did Anyway 16

Whatever it Takes to Fit into Our Calvin Klein Jeans, 1981 17

A Poem is the Chelsea Hotel 18

Before My Big Brother's Casket Closes 19

Palinode 20

Elegy with Shadows and Light 21

Blades 22

The Lonely Girl 24

The Golden Years 25

Ritual Lost 26

Self-Portrait Told by Things That Don't Suck 27

daughters

The Father Drives Me Home
for Ella

I slide into the passenger seat,
where his wife usually sits.

He seems so old. Thirty-two, thirty-three,
compared to my thirteen.

It starts with questions as we glide
down the street. He asks about

my winning soccer team, and which boy
in class is my biggest crush.

His hand sweeps my knee as he promises
that boy would be lucky to have me.

He brushes my breast as he draws his hand
back to the wheel. So soft, so subtle,

I tell myself it must be a mistake.

He turns the car into an empty Target parking lot,
apologizes for forgetting the toddler needs milk

for tomorrow's Frosted Flakes, hopes it's okay
that our ride home is delayed. He reaches

over my lap to open the door, to show how gentlemanly
he can be, I suppose. Then stops, takes a moment to thank me

for caring for his baby girl, reading her *Goodnight Moon*,
telling her that Mom and Dad will be home soon.

He presses his fingers between my thighs.
I cross my legs, push my chest against

the door and close my eyes.

Waiting for My Father in the Lobby of the Disneyland Hotel

I waited all night on a paisley
print sofa by a statue of Pooh,
while Mom dropped quarters
into a payphone frantically
searching for you. I pulled
a velvet pillow to my chest,
its softness roughed up
by years of tired parents,
toddlers' sticky shoes
and salesmen passing through.
You said you'd be back at six.
Promised you'd balance me
on your knee as we wound
through tunnels of the Caribbean,
crack bad jokes as thieves chase
sassy maidens 'round and 'round,
and the junkyard dog held
the jailer's key between his teeth.
You promised to dry my lashes
with your sleeve after we splashed
down the last fall. Then celebrate
our voyage with meatloaf and Shirley Temples
at The Blue Bayou.

       But you never came back,
not that day, anyway.

We finally found you in the card room
down the road, lighting a Lucky Strike
as you raised your last poker hand.
You didn't see us watch you throw
your cards on the floor, flick ashes
in the winner's eyes, cut your fists
on glass as you punched your way
out the door.

My First Name is Margaret

It means pearl.
I have never cared
for pearls.
Their soft round
shape, silky
white glaze.
Usually bound
by a string,
wrapped around
a neck.

Wikipedia says
pearls
are accidents
created
when an intruder
settles inside
a shell
at the bottom
of the sea.
It could be
a grain of sand,
or a lost particle
drifting in unseen.

Wild pearls
are rare.
Hundreds
of oysters
must be gathered
and killed
to find
one perfect
gem.

I wish
I had asked
my mother
why
she named me
after such
a rare seed.

Did I, the youngest
baby, unexpected,
unexplained,
conceived
when she thought
she was free,
break through
her skin
like a parasite
feeding
on her dreams.

Maybe that's
why I never
loved my name.
I could never
live up to its
grace.
I could never
know
my beauty,
know
my value,
knowing
my mother
gave up
her life,
so I could
have mine.

Ode to My Father's Marlboro Lights

I knew my father was home
by the stench of his Marlboro Lights.

Waking in the middle of the night
to smoke snaking through walls,

his breath scratching my skin
through my bedroom door,
latched from the inside.

Embers flickering on a dish
warned me to walk softly,

to slip out of the room, unseen.
To stifle my words, cover my glare.

The strike of his match meant
he was staying a while.

Poker games, whiskey, passing out
in his La-Z-Boy chair.

Looking back, I am thankful
for the flares.

Though I was choking,
at least I knew where he was.

I could avoid his fire,
avoid being burned.

When I Was Sixteen, I Realized My Parents Were No Longer In Love

It dawns with the morning sheets
pulled tight around the corners.

The blankets still folded
at the foot of the bed.

One pillow hollowed in the middle,
the other billowed perfectly,

like a newborn cloud.
I tell myself not to worry.

This must be how
married couples sleep.

Her slim hips line up with his,
her breasts rest on his chest

as he pulls satin sheets over
her back. His arms sweep

her shoulders, warm hands
glide down her spine.

They share their love, quiet
and sweet. Bodies still,

so a house full of children
won't lose a good night's sleep.

The Day My Mother Disappeared

*In the 1970s, the Baker Act made it possible for a husband to commit
his wife to "a hospital," with little proof of mental illness.*

A white van pulls up to our house.
Red letters and a cross on each side.

My mother doesn't fight as four men,
larger than my father, walk her out,

their hands clawed around her arms.

Her hair tucked beneath her fuchsia
scarf, tied in a knot under her chin.

Eyes hidden behind dark glasses,
I can't see her tears.

I wonder if she can see mine
as they drive off, Mom locked in the back.

Dad tells us she is resting
in a place with sunshine and starched

sheets. She will get lots of sleep.
Come back happy. Smiling and sweet.

Nice people will give her medicine
and teach her homemaking skills.

She'll do yoga, sing songs, stroll
the garden, walk off her pain.

It's a husband's duty to take care of his wife,
my father explains.

The Snow Globe

I forgot about waking up, your coat
missing from the rack, coffee cup

scrubbed clean in the sink, Cadillac
nowhere to be found. I forgot the empty

seat at the head of the table, Mom
calling you at 6:00 Mountain Time,

handing me the phone, kissing you
through the line. I forgot meeting

you at the door every Friday night,
digging through your suitcase

for a snow globe from a city far away.
I forgot the smell of whiskey staining

your lap, cigarettes scorching fabric
as they fell on the floor. I forgot

the sound of your voice pounding
through walls, Mom's whispers begging

you to stop, her blood-stained fingers
from scratching at your arms, silence

the next morning, her eyes plump
and confused.

I forgot jumping into your arms,
pleading for you to stay,

staring into the tiny forest,
white flakes flowing in glass,

loving and hating you,
holding both in my hands.

Our Apartment Downtown

Didn't have curtains,
it had sheets
draped over glass.
It didn't have bedframes,
it had mattresses
flopped on the floor.
It didn't have a washing machine,
it had yellowed bras
soaking in the tub.
It didn't have air conditioning,
it had windows jarred open
all night.
It didn't have toilet paper,
it had newspaper
scrunched into balls.
It didn't have a telephone,
it had dimes collecting
in a can.
It didn't have lamps,
it had lightbulbs
hanging on wires.
It didn't have quiet,
it had our palms
pressed over our ears.
It didn't have peace,
we found that in our mother's eyes.
It didn't have joy
we found that in her stories.
It didn't have a father,
but it had our mom.

My Champion

When I feel like a victim of life,
I hold a photo of my mother in my mind.

Sitting tall on our tenement's step.
Four daughters sharing her lap.

Three sons shoving their way into the frame.
Her hands wrapped around my waist.

Nails ripped by hours scrubbing pans.
Arms scarred by burnt coffee and bacon grease.

I remember her uniform torn on the side,
knees bleeding through her tights,

feet swollen and red. Eyes tired, asking for sleep.
I remember watching her sink into the tub

after another twelve-hour shift, wincing
as the heat rippled over her skin. Yet,

she never pushed us off her lap,
or turned her cheek away from our lips.

For Eight Weeks

you kept
me company.

Never any
trouble

I could feel
your dreams

growing inside
of me

I imagined the curl
of your nose

the tilt
of your smile

the feather
of your skin

the silk
of your hair

resting
on my breast

stories
I would sing

while swaying
you to sleep.

Then one day
a smear of red

like a lily pad

floating
away.

sisters

Benefits of Being the Black Sheep

No need to pack the trunk
of my burnt orange Mustang
in the dark breaths of a peeking
flashlight. No need to creak
away in the stir of morning,
or back out with my motor
sound asleep. No need to creep
down 3rd Street until the echo
of my ignition feigns the rumble
of the first train leaving Main
Station. No one will parade
after me. The lift of his drunken
brow, and her half-asleep grumble,
my only goodbyes.
I'll careen down I-10 into my life,
watching potholes, 7-Elevens,
churches and half a dozen
schools that raised me
disappear into oblivion.

Self-Portrait in Things My Sisters Told Me Not to Do, but I Did Anyway

Dye my hair black. Walk alone
after dark. Run away from home.
Never go back. Live in the city.
Squeeze into that leather miniskirt.
Wear eyeliner to bed. Sleep with
the windows open. Drink coffee
at midnight. Sip wine
and whiskey at the same time.
Eat chocolate for breakfast, French
toast for dinner. Bite my nails.
Chew my bottom lip. Break string
with my teeth. Say *fuck*. Run
the New York City Marathon, then
run it again. Quit school to be on TV.
Quit my family to survive. Go to therapy.
Stay in therapy. Call the police
when my brother sold cocaine. Forgive
my mother. Forgive my father.
Do a back flip off the high dive
when I was 33. Stop on the edge
of the 405 to catch that dog
running along the metro tracks. Fall in love
on the first date. Marry the man I fell in love
with on the first date. Ignore their calls.

Whatever it Takes to Fit into Our Calvin Klein Jeans, 1981

Happiness hinges on hips that twist
into Calvin Klein jeans, size zero.

Strutting like a fevered Saturday night,
we prance past boys, chins cocked

over our shoulders like Brooke Shields
shows us how to do. Ruby-tipped

fingernails tucked in back pockets,
thumbs dangling on denim's edge,

brushing our butts with each exaggerated
sway. Sixteen-year-old virgins playing the part,

practicing the moves of Hollywood starlets,
roller disco queens, and adulterous

young wives our moms chatter about
over Virginia Slims and whiskey-spiked tea.

Cake make-up hides our zits, Aqua Net
holds our feathered hair. Our favorite pair

of CKs, begged for on birthday gift lists,
holds our dreams. Our reward for salad bar

lunches, grapefruit diets, barfing up Taco
Bell and Twinkies when we have a bad day.

Friendships are built on Friday nights.
Kitchen forks gripped in our fists, lanky

bodies splayed across silky bedspreads,
a team of teenage girls working together

to force the gold-plated zipper   up, up, up
until the magical   click!

A Poem is the Chelsea Hotel
after Bukowski

A poem is a hotel bed,
with stained sheets,
and bras twisted under silk.

It's the housekeeper counting
her tips, receptionist singing
the blues. It's portraits of dead

artists glaring at strangers
slinking up stairs, haunted
eyes following them to their doors.

A poem is marble floors bruised
by the boots of Schuyler, Thomas,
Cohen, Vicious, Smith and Mapplethorpe.

It's lyrics whispered into smoke,
lines scratched on envelope flaps,
pages crumpled in the trash,
chapters aborted in the dark.

A poem is face-slapping arguments
between lovers, poets coughing
up blood, blowjobs given
by fallen rock stars.

A poem is punks, pockmarked
and pale, shooting heroin
on the toilet tile. Knives thrust
into hearts. Fashion models
shivering on the roof, barefoot,
and alone.

Before My Big Brother's Casket Closes

I wear my red dress,
with black buttons,
and lace on the sleeves.
He always told me
it made me look pretty,
like a Hollywood star.

The gold-plated coin
we panned for together
at Knott's Berry Farm
is tucked in my lap.
We made a wish on
the others, tossed
them back into the stream.
But this one. This one
he slipped into my pocket
to carry good luck.

I squeeze through the pews,
past knees and adult feet
to the aisle where my brother's
widow waits for me.
She slides her fingers into mine,
ties them up like a knot.
I tremble as we walk
to the casket.
I peek over the edge,
to study his face,
so I don't forget.

I kiss our coin,
drop it in,
wish him luck.

They shut the lid.

Palinode

for my sister

Stop pretending
he was by your side,
you were sound asleep.
You didn't see him
shuffle to the door, hear
his feet creaking the floor
his hand turning the knob
his breath piercing my lips
his palm pushing my mouth,
his knees pressing my hips,
my elbow banging the wall,
my cries muffled under his moans.

My smile isn't real, my tears aren't
from joy, and you're not innocent
of his crimes.

Elegy with Shadows and Light
for Shanon

We linger on the edge of her bed,
as ribbons of sun float in from the lake.
Uninvited cells have stolen her sight,
but she can feel the warmth on her lids,
the heat casting amber through her hair.
As our lives melt together one last time,
we tear-up over twenty years wasting
summer days in bargain bikinis, sunburning
for hours because we just don't care.
Blowing kisses to college boys across
the pond, splashing away when they shoot
kisses back. Losing our virginity to football
players we tell ourselves we love,
vowing never to speak of our mistakes.
Drinking Boone's Farm until we can't
stand, fighting off the last August night.
When Labor Day pulls us back to life,
we promise to walk our separate paths
together, never let silences tear us apart.
As the room turns grey, her fingers
slide into mine.

Blades

for Jerry

From the fold of his elbow
    to the curve

of his nails, purple and ash
    bracelet his wrists,

smoke and blood tattoo
    his veins. Blurred pictures:

my hands pressing his
    wounds, pounding his chest. My lips

blowing life into his lungs, waiting
    for a trembling lip, a flickering lid,

a gasping breath,
    a voice whispering I want to live.

I dig for an unsent letter
    under unpaid bills, a quavering message begging

for an urgent call back. How did I miss
    lost gazes, meals untouched, forgotten

appointments, tear-soaked tissues tucked in pockets.
    Pain cut so sharp he'd choose dirt and nothing

over coffee walks on Sunday mornings, three o'clock
    bourbon on the beach, counting pigeons at the park,

confessing Friday night lies until we cry,
    locking fingers while we sleep,

holding kisses until we drift into dreams.
    How did I miss his nightmares

and empty days,
    his mind slipping, the blade

hovering-

The Lonely Girl

She wakes in the dark
to an empty room
enveloped in walls
dented by fists.
She stumbles
to the only window,
hidden in the corner,
behind a spider web
and row of steel bars.
She peeks out at the sky.
There's no sign of the moon.
No sign of the stars.
Even they
are afraid of her rage.

The Golden Years

I'm afraid of dying
alone. On soiled sheets.
No one I know
monitoring my morphine
drip. An empty plastic chair.
A black and white TV.
Christmas slumped
in a wheelchair.
Or propped up like a rag
doll, sipping juice
from a Styrofoam cup.
Part-time nurses singing
Jingle Bells. Orderlies wearing
red hats with white pom poms
on their tips, pushing
me through halls lined
with parked gurneys
holding the almost dead.
Wondering as I roll
down the grey corridors
if I should have birthed
a child of my own,
a caretaker, committed
by blood, to give me
a room in her home.
A daughter to fill my
bookshelves with roses
and stacks of Didion
essays, and my twilight
years with grandchildren
who would listen
to my funny stories
and old family lies.
Then I notice Jenny,
grandmother of nine,
dying alone,
just like me.

Ritual Lost
for Corey

For years they walked
together, every morning
at seven a.m.
I'd watch them
from my window,
impressed by their pace.
They never locked hands,
but were always in stride.
Lately, she walks alone.
Her head down, eyes
focused on the road
ahead. She moves slower,
like she is lost, or looking
for something.
I wonder where
he has gone.
I make up stories
to fill the void.
Maybe he's on sabbatical,
learning to sleep in.
Perhaps he flew to Paris,
and is writing a novel
dedicated to her love.
I want to ask,
but I don't dare.
So I turn to mine,
still lying in bed,
I slide in next to him
and take his hand.

Self-Portrait Told by Things That Don't Suck
after Andrea Gibson

Los Angeles in December. Long hair that shines all year round.
The Hollywood sign at dawn. Golden Retrievers covered in mud.
Black boots. Black jackets. Black and white photos of Mom and Dad
from 1943. Coffee with clotted cream. Hepburn and Tracy films.
Gliding toes through wet sand. Jazz on Mondays. Whiskey, neat.
Hotel lobbies with Christmas Trees. Hot soup on a cold porch.
Being followed by your neighbor's cat. Spoons and knives on the right
side, forks on the left. Silk napkins. Jeans fresh out of the dryer.
New York City in November. Leaves landing at your feet. Lady Bugs
landing on your hand. Kisses first thing in the morning. Kisses
last thing at night. Downtown libraries. Birthday cards. Green eyes.
Soft shoulders. Laughs so hard your tummy aches. Airline upgrades.
Paris in April. Grilled cheese sandwiches. A stranger opening the door
for you when your hands are full. Thunderstorms. Delight in a child's
eyes when you hand them cookie mixers to lick. Melted butter.
A deep, long, hard crying session with your best friend. Reading
The New Yorker in a sidewalk café. Holding hands. Seeing a couple
in their nineties still holding hands. Writing poems. A house to
yourself on a rainy day. Candlelit rooms. Saying I love you and
hearing it back. Finding the matching sock.

With Thanks

I am deeply grateful to my teachers Suzi Q. Smith, Andre' O. Hoilette, and Richie Hofmann for sharing their infinite wisdom and grace.

With endless gratitude to my mentors Erin Rodoni and Rebecca Goss, whose honesty, patience and support taught me more than I ever could have imagined. My pages would still be blank without them.

A special thanks to the Southampton Writers Conference for giving this rookie a shot, and for the gift of a beautiful writing community.

Deepest thanks to Billy Collins for living up to his legend (and then some), for sharing his lifetime of poetry wisdom, and for being the funniest teacher I've ever had the honor of sitting across a table from. I'm still laughing.

For their friendship and support, my endless thanks to my cheerleaders Jenny Turnbull, Carla Sarett, Julie Khuzami, and Josh Potter.

Thanks to my dog Chester Blue, for protecting me from evil squirrels and for warming my feet as I write.

My infinite love and gratitude to my husband Corey Mandell, for the bottomless coffee, and for being the best teammate a writer/ wife could ever have.

These poems are for my badass girl heroes: Alli, Judi, Mom, Shanon, Amy and Roxanne.

M.R. Mandell was born in Southern California, then whisked off to Texas, Austria, and Missouri, as a child. A California girl at heart, she ran back to Los Angeles on her eighteenth birthday to chase a career in acting. After a few years, and a collection of one-line gigs on soap operas, sitcoms, and after school specials, she stumbled headfirst into poetry. Her poems have appeared in *The McNeese Review, HAD,* and *Door Is A Jar,* among others. Her debut chapbook, *"Don't Worry About Me,"* was released in 2024 (Bottlecap Press). She attended the Southampton Writers Conference under the mentorship of Billy Collins.

When not writing, she can be found exploring the streets of Hollywood with her muse, a Golden Retriever named Chester Blue, and her husband, also a writer.

www.ingramcontent.com/pod-product-compliance
Lightning Source LLC
LaVergne TN
LVHW090247210925
821548LV00003B/72